STEM
BODY

CLONING
humans

by Leah Kaminski

FAST READS

full tilt
PRESS

Cloning Humans
STEM Body

Full Tilt Press
42964 Osgood Road
Fremont, CA 94539
readfulltilt.com

Full Tilt Press publications may be purchased for educational, business, or sales promotional use.

Editorial Credits
Design and layout by Sara Radka
Edited by Renae Gilles
Copyedited by Nikki Ramsay

Image Credits
Flickr: Jun Seita, 27 (top); Getty Images: Brand X Pictures/Science Photo Library/Seonello
Calvetti, 9, E+/RichLegg, 4, Getty Images News, 9, 28 (left), iStock/abezikus, 18, iStock/
Antiv3D, 15, iStock/berya113, background, iStock/wildpixel, 13, Science Photo Library/
Christoph Burgstedt, cover, 11, Westend61, 14; Newscom: Luis Sevillano, 26 (top); Shutterstock:
Blue Andy, 12, Designua, 15, Drop of Light, 24, Emre Terim, 16, Monkey Business Images, 21,
Nathan Devery, 22, phipatbig, 29, Tatiana Shepeleva, 20, Yurchanka Siarhei, 6, 28 (right);
Wikimedia: Nissim Benvenisty, 8, PuppyEggs, 26 (bottom), The He Lab, 27 (bottom)

ISBN: 978-1-62920-837-4 (library binding)
ISBN: 978-1-62920-849-7 (ePub)

CONTENTS

INTRODUCTION

While many people imagine a future of full-body human clones, almost 50 countries have banned human cloning. Lawmakers fear the process would not be safe.

A body without a brain lies on a table. A dying child is wheeled in. The child and the body on the table are identical. In surgery, the boy's healthy brain is taken out. It is placed in the clone. The clone opens its eyes. Is it the same child? Whole body transplants are not yet possible. But cloning science is moving fast.

Scientists can already clone small parts of people. They can also copy entire animals. This is called **reproductive** cloning. Copying humans is not allowed. But it is possible to change babies before they are born. This is called gene editing. It is closely related to cloning.

A clone is a genetic copy of a **cell** or an entire living thing. Genes are in every cell. Parents pass them to children. Genes control how the **organism** grows. Cloning happens in nature. Identical twins are clones. Scientists can also clone cells, genes, or animals on purpose.

reproductive: having to do with creating new life

cell: a very small part of a living being

organism: a living thing

Growing ORGANS

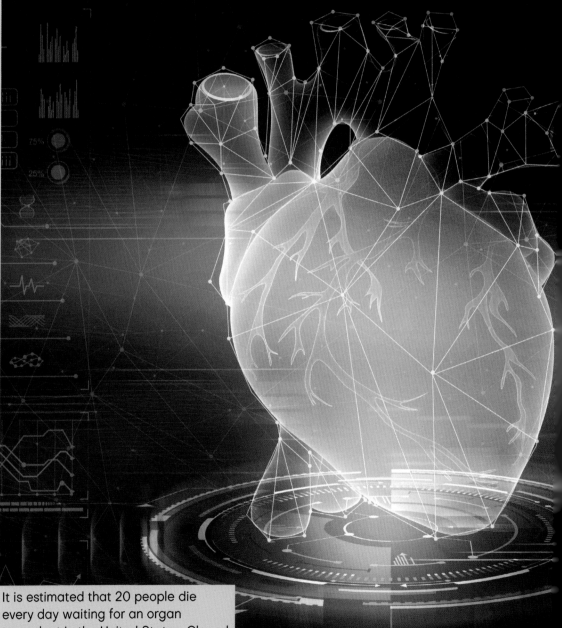

It is estimated that 20 people die every day waiting for an organ transplant in the United States. Cloned organs could help solve this problem.

Scientists can clone animal cells, including human cells. It is called **therapeutic** cloning. One method is called SCNT. That stands for "**somatic** cell nuclear transfer." SCNT helps scientists clone cells. Cloned cells are put into a patient. They treat disease.

There are many future possibilities for SCNT. One is making cloned organs from a patient's own cells.

A cloned organ would be very safe. The organ would match a patient's body. There would be no rejection. Rejection is when the body attacks something. It thinks the intruder does not belong. Rejection is a common and dangerous reaction to organ transplants.

therapeutic: having to do with health and healing

somatic: having to do with the body rather than the mind

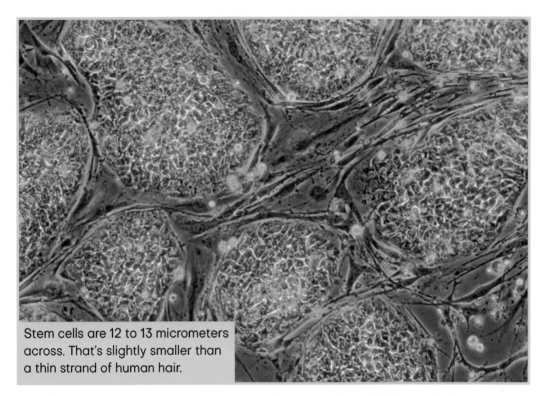

Stem cells are 12 to 13 micrometers across. That's slightly smaller than a thin strand of human hair.

Cloning an organ would start with one cell. SCNT would be used. In SCNT, a scientist takes a tiny needle. They pull out the cell's **nucleus**. They place it in a mother's egg cell. The changed egg cell is shocked. This is done with electricity or special chemicals. The cell begins dividing. Each new cell is a clone. These clones are **stem cells**. Stem cells are unique. They can turn into any of the 200 kinds of human cells. This includes organ cells.

Once there are about 150 stem cells, they can be taken out. Scientists are on their way to growing organs from this kind of stem cell. The organ would form from a clone of the original cell. The patient's body would accept it as its own.

nucleus: the center of a cell, which contains genetic material

stem cell: a simple cell that can become any type of specialized cell, such as a blood cell or a skin cell

SCNT has been used for decades to clone animal cells. It even makes whole animals, such as farm animals.

Scientists in Oregon were the first to use SCNT on human cells. In 2013, they used SCNT. They turned a skin cell into a stem cell.

In theory, SCNT could be used to bring extinct species, such as woolly mammoths, back to life.

Cloning Animals

Dolly the sheep was the first living **mammal** cloned using an adult body cell. Scientists were changing animals in order to make medicine. Cloning the animals would make things easier.

Dolly was born in 1996. She had children and lived like a normal sheep. But Dolly died young, because her genes were from the cells of an adult sheep. Scientists are still trying to find out how to keep cloned animals alive longer.

mammal: a warm-blooded animal with hair or fur that gives birth to live young and feeds its young milk

SCNT

SCNT was developed by experts from many STEM fields. This complex cloning work relies on knowledge from several disciplines.

SCIENCE

A deep knowledge of cell biology was necessary for scientists to develop the ability to clone cells. Many of the people who work in cloning have college degrees in cell biology.

TECHNOLOGY

In order to remove the nucleus from a cell, scientists use specialized technology. An inverted microscope, UV light, and a tiny glass needle are used.

ENGINEERING

Besides genetic engineers, SCNT also relies on mechanical engineers. These people design the machines and instruments used in the process.

MATH

Scientists working with cells use small-scale math. They do calculations with units such as micrometers and micrograms.

Gene THERAPY

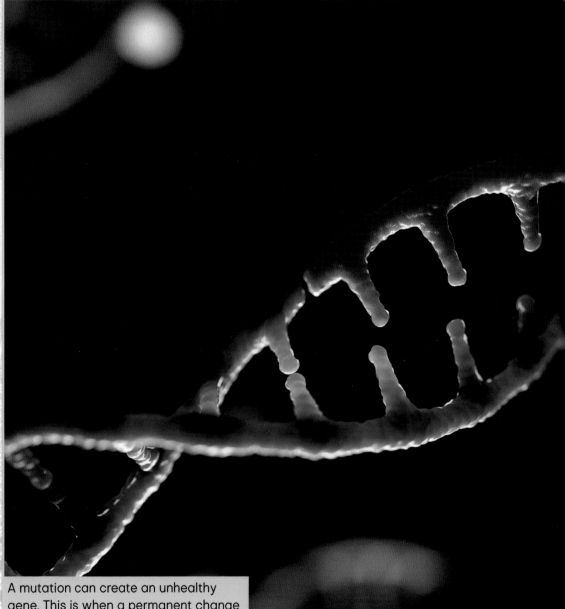

A mutation can create an unhealthy gene. This is when a permanent change is made to the gene. It is usually due to an error during growth or damage from something like too much sun.

Some diseases are caused by unhealthy genes. Gene therapy can help. Drugs are not needed. Surgery is not required either. Gene therapy already helps with blindness. It cures a dangerous blood disease. Someday gene therapy might be used to cure cancer.

Gene therapy uses gene cloning. It is different than therapeutic cloning. Single genes are cloned, not whole cells. Genes are only a small part of a cell. Gene cloning is also used to make medicines. They help treat cancer and diabetes.

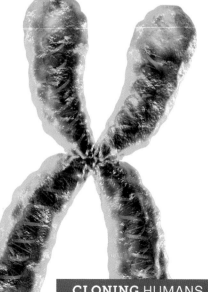

Scientists think every human has from 20,000 to 25,000 genes. Each gene makes up a small section of a DNA strand.

In gene therapy, doctors find an unhealthy gene. The gene stops cells from working correctly. It causes disease. A healthy copy of the gene is cloned. It is put into cells. The cells work again.

The first gene cloning was in the 1970s. To clone genes, human **DNA** is used. Scientists find the gene they want. They cut the DNA into pieces. A special chemical does this. DNA from bacteria is also cut into pieces. The human and bacterial DNA are mixed. They combine. It is then called **recombinant** DNA. It is put into living bacteria. The bacteria grow. The gene is now cloned.

Cells and DNA

Cell

Chromosome

DNA

Gene

Gene therapy uses the cloned gene. The cloned gene is mixed with a patient's cells. Scientists are still learning the best way to mix genes with cells.

The first gene therapy was done in 1990. In 2017, the United States approved its first gene therapy. It was for cancer. By 2019, there were more gene therapies approved.

DNA: a material in the cells of plants and animals that carries genetic information

recombinant: made by scientists mixing genetic material

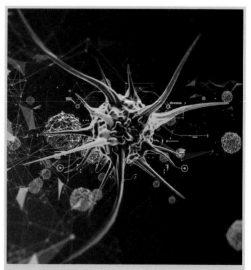

In gene therapy, viruses can be used as "taxis" to carry genes into a patient's body.

GENE CLONING

Recombinant DNA is created through gene cloning. This technique is widely used in many STEM fields.

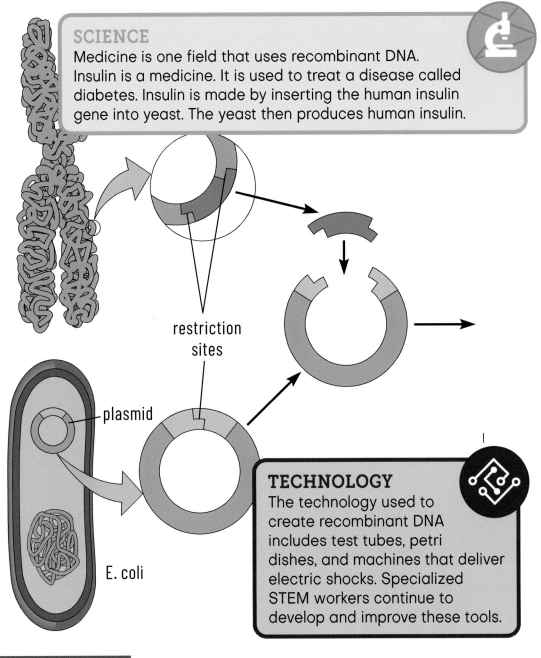

SCIENCE
Medicine is one field that uses recombinant DNA. Insulin is a medicine. It is used to treat a disease called diabetes. Insulin is made by inserting the human insulin gene into yeast. The yeast then produces human insulin.

restriction sites

plasmid

E. coli

TECHNOLOGY
The technology used to create recombinant DNA includes test tubes, petri dishes, and machines that deliver electric shocks. Specialized STEM workers continue to develop and improve these tools.

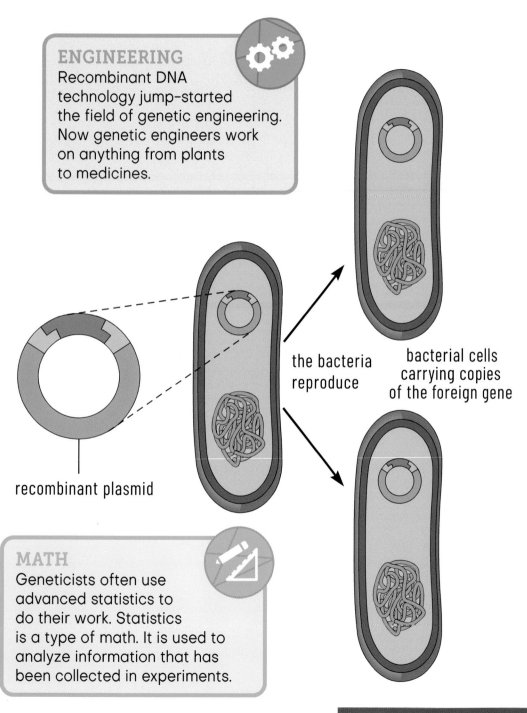

recombinant plasmid

the bacteria reproduce

bacterial cells carrying copies of the foreign gene

Designer BABIES

More than 1 million people have been born in the United States since 1987 through the use of IVF and other processes.

To make a baby, a father's sperm enters a mother's egg and **fertilizes** it. This creates an embryo, which then grows into a baby. Sometimes this process does not work on its own. In this case, embryos can be made outside of a mother's body. They are implanted. This is called in-vitro fertilization (**IVF**).

Now the best embryo can be chosen based on its genes. This is called PGS. PGS is used when both parents have an **inherited** disease or condition. It is also used to choose if the baby will be a boy or girl. Parents can pick eye color too. Some call a child grown from this kind of embryo a "designer baby."

An embryo's genes can even be changed. This is called gene editing. PGS and gene editing are closely related to therapeutic and gene cloning. They are all forms of **biotechnology**. They each try to control how new organisms are created, at the DNA level.

Cloning is also used together with gene editing. For example, scientists edited the genes of monkeys. They gave them genetic diseases. Then they cloned the monkeys. That way they can study the diseases more easily.

fertilize: to make an egg able to grow and develop into a new organism

IVF: when an egg is fertilized in a lab and then implanted into the mother's body to grow

inherit: to receive from a parent

biotechnology: using living cells to make useful products

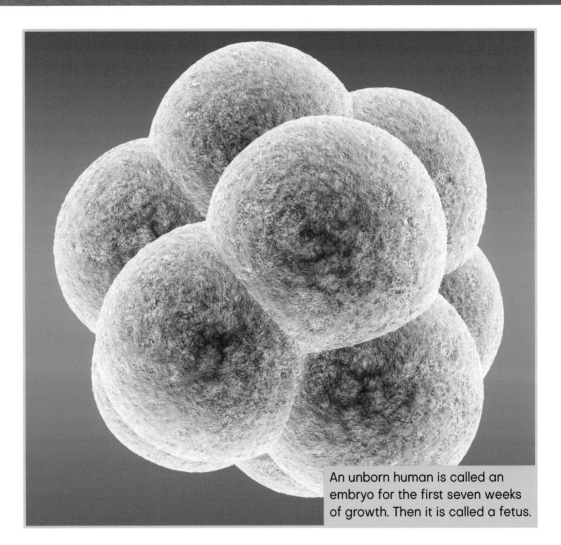

An unborn human is called an embryo for the first seven weeks of growth. Then it is called a fetus.

Gene editing changes an embryo's genes. It has only been done once. Chinese twins with edited genes were born in 2018. A new technique called CRISPR made this easier.

For gene editing, genes are put into the sperm and egg cells. They can also be put into the embryo. Every cell of the resulting baby is changed by this. Every **descendant** of that baby is also changed.

descendant: a person or other living creature who is related to another who lived in the past

The Ethics of Designer Babies

In general, people think **germline** engineering is okay if it prevents disease. But it could possibly be used to make "super babies." These children could be healthier or more beautiful than others. People believe that it would be unfair for this kind of use. It's possible that only wealthy people could afford it. This would make society less equal. This may never become a problem, though. It will probably be very difficult for scientists to select for **traits** such as intelligence or athleticism. These traits are complex. They come from multiple genes and from a child's **environment**.

Gene editing has already been used with IVF. Scientists think that some **infertility** comes from a problem with genes. The problem is in a part of a mother's egg cells. To fix it, the nucleus of her egg cell is placed inside another woman's healthy egg. This new egg is fertilized. The resulting child has the genes of two mothers and one father. This practice is banned in the United States. Lawmakers are worried that it would lead to more and more gene editing. They do not believe it is right for that to happen.

germline: specialized cells that can pass DNA on to the next generation

trait: a quality or characteristic that makes one thing different from another

environment: the conditions that influence someone or something and affect its development or growth

infertility: the state of being unable to reproduce

CRISPR

Researchers have only recently begun to edit human genes. CRISPR technology made it much easier for scientists to do this work.

D

SCIENCE

A Spanish biologist was behind the breakthrough CRISPR technology. He discovered the bacteria that defended itself by cutting DNA.

Cas9

TECHNOLOGY

A bacteria, not a machine, does the work of gene editing with CRISPR. That's part of what makes the technology so groundbreaking.

DNA—

ENGINEERING

Genetic engineers use what they call "molecular scissors" to remove and replace genes. CRISPR is one such set of engineered enzymes.

MATH

Mathematicians found a way to model how to predict the errors that CRISPR might make in cutting DNA. This will help avoid dangerous mistakes.

—RNA

The Cloning
COMMUNITY

The United Nations created a committee in 2001. Its purpose was to look at potential issues with cloning and human safety.

Scientists must do their work. But they cannot do anything they want. It is important to agree on rules. Some people do not want to clone embryos. They think it is wrong. Some scientists worry about cloned stem cells. They might grow out of control. They might act like cancer cells. The results of gene therapy and gene editing are unknown.

China does not have many rules about cloning. Chinese scientists can try many things. They make breakthroughs. In April 2015, Chinese scientists made a major report. They were the first to try editing a human embryo.

After this, some countries stopped human gene editing. They also stopped scientists from changing DNA. They could only do it if it cured a disease. But many practices are still allowed. In 2017, the US National Academy of Sciences said they support using CRISPR to cure diseases in embryos. There will be much progress in the future.

CLONING SCIENTISTS

STEM workers from around the world are leading the way in cloning science.

SHOUKHRAT MITALIPOV

Shoukhrat Mitalipov is an expert in therapeutic cloning. In 2007, he used SCNT on a monkey's cell. Then in 2013, he made human stem cells with SCNT. It was the first time this had been done. In 2017, he was one of many to use CRISPR to edit human embryos.

FENG ZHANG

Feng Zhang was the first scientist to show that CRISPR could edit the DNA in human cells. Zhang is calling for scientists not to use CRISPR to create babies. He says the risks are greater than the benefits.

HIROMITSU NAKAUCHI

Hiromitsu Nakauchi is a biologist. In 2019, Japan allowed him to start working with human–animal embryos. Nakauchi wants to grow human organs in animals. He will put **hybrid** embryos into animals and grow them. The organs will be taken out and used in human patients.

HE JIANKUI

He Jiankui is a Chinese scientist. He changed the embryos of two Chinese twins, Lulu and Nana. Jiankui edited a gene using CRISPR. He tried protecting the girls against HIV. The twins were born in 2018. It is unclear if the experiment worked. Jiankui did his work secretly. Many scientists question whether this was right.

---

hybrid: the offspring of two animals or plants of different kinds

QUIZ

1 Is copying humans allowed?

2 Does cloning happen in nature?

3 Why would a cloned organ be very safe?

4 Why did Dolly the sheep die young?

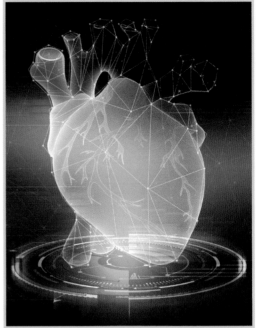

5 What does SCNT stand for?

6 When was the first gene therapy done?

7 What is it called when an embryo's genes are changed?

8 Who was the first scientist to show that CRISPR could edit the DNA in human cells?

ACTIVITY
Create a Mind Map

Choose one of the concepts discussed in this book. Which one interests you most? Learn more about it through research, a mind map, and help from an adult.

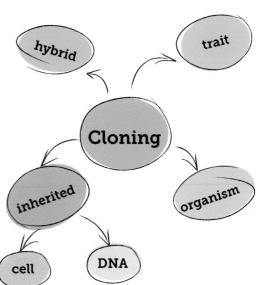

STEPS

1. Do a search for your chosen concept online. Read some news articles and some kids' websites.

2. Now that you know more, draw a mind map. Put your main concept in a big bubble in the middle of the paper. Organize your new information around it.

3. Based on your mind map, write a list of questions. Where are the gaps in your understanding? What do you want to know more about?

4. Ask an adult to help you find a researcher at a nearby college. Contact them to ask your questions. Or ask a research librarian to help you find answers in a book.

5. Ask your teacher if you can present your findings in class. Or set up a lecture at home.

GLOSSARY

biotechnology: using living cells to make useful products

cell: a very small part of a living being

descendant: a person or other living creature who is related to another who lived in the past

DNA: a material in the cells of plants and animals that carries genetic information

environment: the conditions that influence someone or something and affect its development or growth

fertilize: to make an egg able to grow and develop into a new organism

germline: specialized cells that can pass DNA on to the next generation

hybrid: the offspring of two animals or plants of different kinds

infertility: the state of being unable to reproduce

inherit: to receive from a parent

IVF: when an egg is fertilized in a lab and then implanted into the mother's body to grow

mammal: a warm-blooded animal with hair or fur that gives birth to live young and feeds its young milk

nucleus: the center of a cell, which contains genetic material

organism: a living thing

recombinant: made by scientists mixing genetic material

reproductive: having to do with creating new life

somatic: having to do with the body rather than the mind

stem cell: a simple cell that can become any type of specialized cell, such as a blood cell or a skin cell

therapeutic: having to do with health and healing

trait: a quality or characteristic that makes one thing different from another

READ MORE

Bond, Dave. *Genetic Engineering.* STEM: Shaping the Future. New York: Smartbook Media Inc., 2019.

Hand, Carol. *Reviving Extinct Species.* Sci-Fi or STEM? New York: Rosen Publishing, 2019.

Jackson, Tom. *Is Human Cloning in Our Future?: Theories about Genetics.* Beyond the Theory: Science of the Future. New York: Gareth Stevens Publishing, 2018.

Lew, Kristi. *Human Cloning.* Sci-Fi or STEM? New York: Rosen Publishing, 2019.

Wood, John. *Medical Technology: Genomics, Growing Organs, and More.* STEM in Our World. New York: Gareth Stevens Publishing, 2018.

INTERNET SITES

https://kids.britannica.com/kids/article/cloning/574603
Learn more about cloning with Brittanica Kids.

https://www.sciencenewsforstudents.org/article/animal-clones-double-trouble
Science News for Students talks about the debate around animal cloning.

https://amino.bio/pages/launchedvbio
Try out bioengineering with a game.

https://www.amnh.org/explore/ology/genetics
Explore genetics topics, including cloning, at the Gene Scene.

https://kids.kiddle.co/CRISPR
Learn more about CRISPR, including its structure.

INDEX